Families and their Faiths

Islam in Turkey

Written by Frances Hawker and Leyla Aliçavuşoğlu
Photography by Bruce Campbell

Tulip Books

TULIP BOOKS®

www.tulipbooks.co.uk

This edition published by:
Tulip Books
Dept 302
43 Owston Road
Carcroft
Doncaster
DN6 8DA.

© in this edition Tulip Books 2014
© in text Francis Hawker 2008
© in photographs Bruce Campbell 2008

British Library Cataloguing in Publication Data (CIP) is available for this title.

ISBN: 978-1-78388-015-7

Printed in Spain by Edelvives

Contents

My name is Fatma. I live with my family in a small village by the sea in Turkey. This is me cooking dinner with my grandson, Metehan. I also have a granddaughter called Ayşe.

Every day the family likes to sit together and chat, eat and drink tea. Today we are enjoying fresh fruit, pistachio nuts, dried apricots, Turkish delight and sweets made of figs and walnuts.

Metehan and Ayşe go to school in the village. Our village is tiny. There are only eight children at the school!

The children are learning about the history of Turkey and a famous leader called Ataturk. Some children are writing stories about Ataturk to enter a competition for local schools.

Like most people in Turkey we are Muslims. We follow a religion called Islam. Muslims worship together in a mosque. Once a week the children have lessons at the mosque with the Imam. He is the leader of our mosque. They are learning to read our holy book, the Qur'an.

The Qur'an is written in Arabic. I read it at home every day. It sounds like poetry when it is read aloud. Metehan and Ayşe sometimes listen.

The Qur'an contains important messages for all Muslims.

Muslims pray five times each day. The first
prayer is said before the sun rises. We must wash
before praying. This washing is called *wudu*.
Metehan uses the taps outside the mosque.
He washes his face, hands, arms and feet.
As he washes, he says special prayers.

The act of prayer is called *salah*. We face Mecca and say special prayers in Arabic.

We praise Allah and recite part of the Qur'an.

We pray 'Glory to my Lord the Great.'

We praise Allah and recite more prayers.

We pray for all Muslims and ask for forgiveness.

One afternoon the children meet Uncle Ibrahim. He is a goat herder. 'What do you eat when you are alone in the mountains?' Ayşe asks.

'I drink goat's milk and make yoghurt and cheese. I pick nuts, apples, peaches, and apricots.'

'How do you pray if you are far from a mosque?'

'So many questions! You can pray anywhere. I use a compass to make sure I face Mecca, the holy city.'

Tonight is the start of Ramadan. Ramadan celebrates the time when Allah, our God, revealed the Qur'an to Muhammad. It starts when the new crescent moon is seen, and finishes a month later. Metehan sees it first. 'Come and see the moon. It is above the mosque,' he calls. We all rush to look.

During the holy month of Ramadan, we do not eat or drink between sunrise and sunset to show our love of God. Children fast only if they want to. 'I'll fast for four days,' says Metehan. 'I'll start tomorrow.'

Metehan wakes early to eat breakfast before sunrise. Then he sleeps until Ayşe wakes him. 'Quick, Uncle Mustafa said we can help him deliver bread to the village of Simena.'

They hurry down to the jetty. There is no road to Simena so everything is delivered by boat.

The smell of bread makes Metehan hungry.
Uncle Mustafa offers him some. 'No thanks, I'm
fasting today. Don't tempt me!' Metehan laughs.
'It's not easy, is it?' asks Uncle. 'Imagine being
hungry and thirsty every day. Fasting makes us
remember how lucky we are.'

Later the children see Great-Uncle Hassan picking olives. He tells them about his pilgrimage to the holy city of Mecca.

'Muslims try to go on the pilgrimage once in their lifetime. We ask God for forgiveness and mercy.'

As the children listen Metehan pops a sweet into
his mouth. At once he remembers he is fasting
and quickly spits it out. 'Oh no!' he shouts.

'Do not worry,' says Great-Uncle. 'If you eat or
drink without thinking it does not matter, just go
on with your fast.'

During Ramadan everyone goes to the mosque after dinner. Each night of the month the Imam reads part of the Qur'an.

Women usually pray at home, but during Ramadan we go to the mosque. We pray in an upstairs balcony, separate from the men. Women must cover their whole body except the face, the hands and the feet, when we are praying.

Arabic writing from the Qur'an

Tonight is the greatest night of the year. Muhammad received his first message from Allah on this night. Everyone in the village will go to the mosque, and most will stay all night.

Ayşe stays until past her bedtime and soon falls asleep. Metehan wants to stay all night. He does not dare to close his eyes, even for a minute. He watches Great-Uncle twist his prayer beads.

Metehan fasts again on the last day of Ramadan. 'Hasn't it passed quickly?' Ayşe says.

Metehan laughs, 'Yes, except for the days I fasted. They lasted forever. I'm so hungry even the carrots look good.'

'But you hate carrots,' says Ayşe.

It is market day. Tomorrow the festival of breaking the fast begins. It will last three days. The children buy fruit and vegetables.

Finally Metehan breaks his fast for the last time.
We eat dinner, and then we have fruit and coffee.

A beautiful sound fills the village. It is the call to
prayer. We hurry to the mosque for the last prayers
of Ramadan.

Next day the children wake early and are given
new clothes to celebrate the blessings of Ramadan.
They greet me, and like most grandparents on
this special day, I give my grandchildren money.
They plan how to spend it. They are very excited.

27

The children dress up in their new clothes. Then they visit every house in the village to wish friends and neighbours 'Happy Eid holiday,' and to collect sweets. They bow and kiss the hands of the older people to show respect. By the end of the morning their sweet bags are full.

Many people visit us during the festival. It is a special time to visit friends and relatives, and of course enjoy eating during the day again.

Notes for Parents and Teachers

Muslims follow a religion and a way of life called Islam. They believe in one god, called Allah, who created the universe.

The religion began in the seventh century CE, in what is now Saudi Arabia, when God revealed his message to the prophet Muhammad. Over a period of twenty-three years the messages that make up the Qur'an were revealed to Muhammad through the Angel Gabriel. Over a billion people all over the world now follow Islam.

Pages 6 and 7

In Turkey children are not allowed to wear any religious clothing to school because the government and educational systems are separate from religion. In some Islamic countries schools are run by religious leaders and children must wear religious clothing.

The modern Turkish republic was founded in 1923 by Ataturk, 'Father of the Turks', whose real name was Mustafa Kemal. Ataturk led the Turkish army in defeating invading armies and then went on to become the first president of Turkey.

Metehan is one of the winners of the essay competition (see picture left). He gives a speech on Republic Day, which celebrates the creation of the modern republic. Metehan talks about the way that Ataturk modernised Turkey: he gave more rights to women, changed the style of Turkish writing and separated religion from the government.

Pages 8 and 9

In their lessons the children are learning the practices all Muslims should perform. These are known as the five pillars of Islam. These are:
1. The declaration of faith: There is no god but Allah, and Muhammad is his messenger.
2. Praying five times each day after washing properly.
3. *Zakat*: giving money to those in need.
4. *Hajj*: it is the duty of all Muslims who are fit enough and can afford it to make a pilgrimage or *hajj* to Mecca in Saudi Arabia, the birthplace of the prophet Muhammad.
5. Fasting during the holy month of Ramadan.

Page 10

The children learn about prophets, who were people sent by God to act as messengers and to guide people. Allah revealed the Qur'an to the prophet Muhammad, and also revealed the Torah to the prophet Moses, the psalms to the prophet David, and the Gospel to the prophet Jesus.

Muslims recognise all these books, but they believe that the Qur'an is the last and final book of Allah, and the only book that has not been changed since it was revealed.

Page 11

The act of *wudu* is extremely thorough: Muslims wash their hands, rinse their mouth, sniff water, wash their face, wash their arms to the elbows, their ears, their neck and their feet up to the ankles and even their toes. *Wudu* not only cleans the body but also makes you spiritually clean and ready to pray.

Page 12

Muslims follow a fixed set of actions and words when they pray. They begin by standing with raised hands and saying, 'Allahu Akbar' - 'God is great.' Then they recite passages from the Qur'an, and pray for all Muslims and for the forgiveness of their sins.

Pages 14 and 15

The Islamic calendar is governed by the phases of the moon. Ramadan is the ninth month of the lunar calendar.

Children do not have to fast during Ramadan, however they may choose to do so for a few days during the month. Very old and sick people, pregnant women, labourers and travellers are also excused. For them, Ramadan is still a time to be close to Allah, and remember that he is creator of everything. It is a time to be kind and help other people, and thank Allah for his gift of the Qur'an.

Pages 18 and 19

When they go on the pilgrimage to Mecca, men all wear the same simple white clothing. This is to show that they are all equal in the eyes of God.

Page 20

The Imam reads one thirtieth of the Qur'an each night so that the entire Qur'an is read during the month of Ramadan.

Pages 24 and 25

In Turkey the festival of breaking the fast is called *Seker Bayrami*, which means Sugar Festival. Muslims in many other countries call it *Eid-ul-Fitr*.

During *Seker Bayrami* all Muslims are required to give a small amount of money to those who are less fortunate. By fasting for a month Muslims learn to be more charitable because they know how hard it is to do without. Even small gifts are important. Muhammad taught that half a date given in charity can lead people closer to Paradise.

Glossary

Allah — The Arabic word for God used by all Muslims

Arabic — The language in which the Qur'an was told to Muhammad

Ataturk — The name given to Mustafa Kemal, an important Turkish figure. It means 'Father of the Turks'

Compass — An instrument used for finding directions

Eid — The festival at the end of Ramadan

Fast — To go without food or drink

Mecca — The Islamic holy city in Saudi Arabia, where Muhammad was born

Mosque — A building where Muslims worship

Muhammad — The founder of Islam. Allah revealed the Qur'an to him

Pilgrimage — A journey to a holy place

Qur'an — The holy book of Islam

Salah — The act of prayer practised by Muslims. It describes the five daily prayers

Turkish Delight — A jelly-like Turkish sweet

Wudu — The act of washing before ritual prayer or touching the Qur'an

Index